Beakman's
Book of
Dead Guys
and Gals
of Science

For more information write Andrews and McMeel, a Universal Press Syndicate Company, 4900 Main Street, Kansas City, Missouri 64112.

Based on the TV show "Beakman's World"

Executive Producer:	Mark Waxman
Producer:	Robert Heath
Writing supervised by:	Richard Albrecht & Casey Keller
Written by:	Barry Friedman & Phil Walsh and Mark Waxman
Actors:	

Beakman:	Paul Zaloom
Beakman's lab assistant:	Eliza Schneider, Alanna Ubach
Lester:	Mark Ritts
Penguins:	Alan Barzman and Bert Berdis

Based on "You Can with Beakman & Jax,"
   created by Jok Church
Typography/Book Production: Millie Beard
Illustrations: Peter Georgeson
Produced by becker&mayer!

Library of Congress Cataloging-in-Publication Data

Colombo, Luann
   Beakman's book of dead guys and gals of science : from the hit TV
show "Beakman's World" / written by Luann Colombo.
                              p. cm.
        ISBN 0-8362-7014-2 : $9.95
        1. Scientists—Biography—Juvenile literature. 2. Women
scientists—Biography—Juvenile literature. [1.Scientists.]
I. Title.
Q141.C54   1994
509' .2'2—dc20   94-28541
[B]   CIP
                                      AC

Other "Beakman's World" products
        **Gear Up Your Gray Matter: 50 Questions and Answers
                from the Hit TV Show "Beakman's World"**
        Build with Beakman: Bacteria Farm
        Build with Beakman: Electronic Intercom

BEAKMAN'S BOOK OF DEAD GUYS AND GALS OF SCIENCE

WRITTEN BY LUANN COLOMBO

ILLUSTRATED BY PETER GEORGESON

Andrews and McMeel
A Universal Press Syndicate Company
Kansas City

DEADications:

To inquisitive young scientists everywhere.

No acknowledgment would be complete without an appreciation of my wonderful parents Lou and Rosemary Colombo, without whom I wouldn't even exist.

Many thanks to Mary Gosslee, D.C., Timothy Evans, M.D. Ph.D., Ron Gregg, Ph.D., Jok Church, The Maria Mitchell Association, Jim Becker, Emily Hall, and Ed Mast, for their contributions to accuracy, brevity, and humor. Big hugs to Conn McQuinn, my guardian angel.

Special thanks to Pierre D. Mourad, Ph.D.—my working physicist friend who willingly imparted his scientific expertise with humility and grace.

Contents

Welcome! The scientists you are about to investigate have many things in common. The first is that they are all dead; stone cold, never to walk the earth again. However, since they have become quite famous, their scientific contributions live on forever (and that's why they're in this book). Each has affected our lives in unique ways, and they were able to make their contribution because of the work of others before them. As Sir Isaac Newton so well said: "If I have seen further it is by standing on the shoulders of giants."

It's not that life is so short, it's just that we're dead for so long.

It would be great, for example, to give Philo T. Farnsworth total credit for inventing the television. But, before Farnsworth could work with picture tubes, he needed the early successes of Galileo with the scientific method; Franklin with electricity; Edison with the phonograph; Bell with sound traveling over a wire; and Newton's insight that white light is made up of all colors. Many inventors made Farnsworth's work possible. As you read, see how many dead scientists you find in other scientist's chapters.

Let's go wake up the dead and see why they're so famous now—and what their lives were like then.

Name: Nicolaus Copernicus
Born: February 14, 1473; Torun, Poland
DEAD: May 24, 1543
Famous because: He was the first astronomer to claim that the earth rotates around the sun.

BORN
1473

1490

1491 Studies astronomy at University of Krakow in Poland.

1497 Observes his first eclipse. Becomes a clergyman of the cathedral, which gives him lifelong financial security and a connection to the Catholic Church. Because of this connection, church officials disagree with his ideas, but he doesn't get in trouble (later, you'll see what happens to Galileo).

Copernicus, a Polish monk, was a really brave guy. He dared to challenge the thirteen-century-old belief that the earth was the center of the universe. He attempted to make people believe that the earth rotated around the sun.

Copernicus's other theory had to do with why things fall to the ground (Newton wasn't around yet to explain gravity). Aristotle had taught that things fall to their "natural place," the center of the universe, which he believed to be earth. If the center of the universe was the sun, a new theory had to be developed. Copernicus's groundwork eventually lead to Newton's theories of gravity.

Ever wonder what truths we currently believe will be disproved some day?

1540
Copernicus finally agrees to the publication of his complete works, On the *Revolutions of the Celestial Spheres*. His editor writes an introduction to the book in order to have the book accepted by the Catholic Church and keep Copernicus out of big trouble. The introduction says that all the ideas in the book were hypothetical guesses and were more of a mathematical exercise than a description of the real thing. Nevertheless, the Catholic Church censors the book from 1616 to 1835.

1503 By now Copernicus has mastered everything there is to know about math, astronomy, and medicine, which, at this point in time, isn't much. He spends the rest of his life trying to disprove what is thought to be fact by the rest of the world.

DEAD

| 1500 | 1510 | 1520 | 1530 | 1540 |

1501 Briefly stops in Germany to claim his position with the Catholic Church, then splits for Italy to study and give lectures.

1510–1514 The Copernican Revolution. Copernicus develops the theory that many planets, including the earth, revolve around the sun. This is called a sun-centered or heliocentric theory. This is in direct contrast to the policy of the Roman Catholic Church, which held that the earth is the center of the universe and that all celestial bodies revolve around it.

1543 A finished copy of his book is brought to Copernicus on the day of his death. It's a real knockout; it does him in.

Copernicus dies never knowing he was right. He did his calculations without the aid of a telescope. Galileo was the first to use a telescope to study the stars, but he wasn't born until 21 years after Copernicus's death.

AS THE PLANET SPINS

Let's look at a globe. The equator is the imaginary line that goes around the middle of the earth. Above the equator is the **Northern Hemisphere.** Below is the **Southern Hemisphere.**

The earth is tilted about 23.5 degrees and spins around on its axis, an imaginary stick that goes from the **North Pole** to the **South Pole.**

It takes twenty-four hours (one day) for the earth to rotate completely on its axis. We don't feel the movement because we're spinning right along with it.

A planet's orbit is the path it takes as it revolves around the sun. It takes 365.26 days (one year) for the earth, in its orbit, to travel completely around the sun.

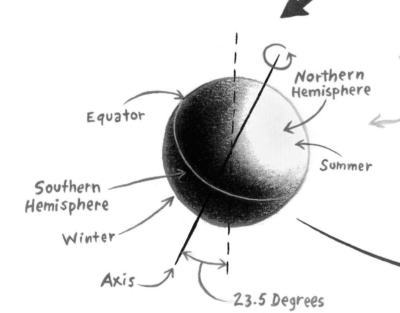

Equator

Northern Hemisphere

Summer

Southern Hemisphere

Winter

Axis

23.5 Degrees

REASONS FOR SEASONS

Sometimes the Southern Hemisphere is pointed toward the sun and other times the Northern Hemisphere is pointed toward the sun. When the earth is in the position shown here in its orbit around the sun, it's summer in the Northern Hemisphere and you don't have to go to school. There are more direct rays of sunlight shining on the northern half of the earth. There are low, slanting rays of sunlight down on the Southern Hemisphere, where it's winter. And when the Southern Hemisphere is tilted toward the sun and the Northern Hemisphere is tilted away, it's summer down south and winter up north.

ASTRONOMY

Astronomy, the study of stars and galaxies, has greatly advanced since the days of Copernicus. For hundreds of years, people really believed the earth was the center of the universe and that the sun and all the stars revolved around it. This time period was called, appropriately, the Dark Ages.

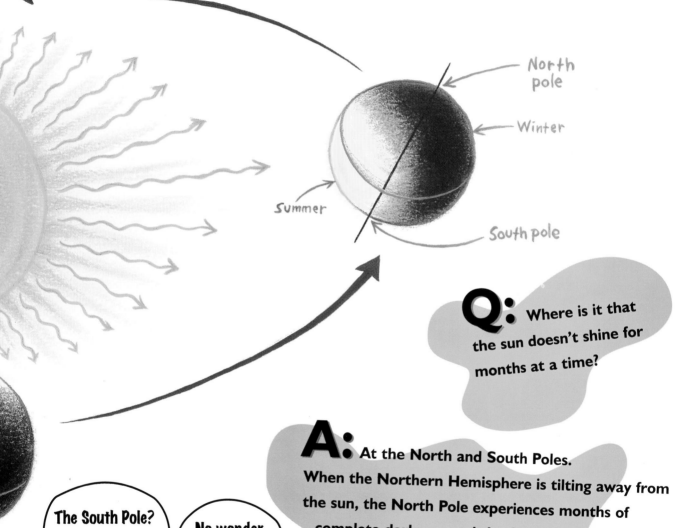

North pole

Winter

South pole

Summer

Q: Where is it that the sun doesn't shine for months at a time?

A: At the North and South Poles. When the Northern Hemisphere is tilting away from the sun, the North Pole experiences months of complete darkness and the South Pole experiences months of constant light. But when the Southern Hemisphere is tilting away from the sun, it's dark at the South Pole and the North Pole has daylight around the clock.

The South Pole? That's where we live!

No wonder it's so dark all winter!

11

Galileo Galilei
Born: February 15, 1564; Pisa, Italy
DEAD: January 8,1642
Famous because: Invented the telescope and was arrested for claiming that the earth travels around the sun, instead of the other way around.

BORN
1564

1580

1590

1582 Galileo closely observes the swing of a chandelier which leads to his work with pendulums and clocks.

1585 Money runs out and Galileo leaves University of Pisa without a degree. Doesn't want to be a doctor. Math and science interest him more.

1592 Becomes professor of mathematics in Padua, Italy.

G alileo was born in Italy at a time when science was based on the teachings of the ancient Greek philosophers, such as Aristotle. These philosophers didn't have a lot of factual information on which to base their beliefs. Galileo was constantly questioning and rejecting scientific findings that hadn't been proven by experiment. His discoveries led him to believe that some of the findings of the ancient Greeks were wrong. His observations allowed him to prove Copernicus's theory that the earth rotates around the sun and is not stationary at the center of the universe, as was taught by the ancient Greeks. To question these beliefs was to deny the word of God. Galileo's discoveries got him in deep trouble with the Catholic Church. He was put on trial before the Inquisition (the court of the Church) in Rome and sentenced to house arrest for the last eight years of his life.

1610

A big year for astronomy. Galileo used the telescope to study the sky. He demonstrated it from the tower of St. Mark's Church in Venice, gaining himself international fame. The telescope was actually first made by someone else, but Galileo improved it and was the first to use it to study the planets, so he gets credit for inventing it.

Here's what he found:

- Venus has phases just like our moon does—from a slim crescent to a full disc.

- Jupiter has four moons, known—due to the discoverer—as Galilean moons: Io, Europa, Ganymede, and Callisto.

- There are three bodies around Saturn. Galileo thought it was a triple planet (whatever that is), but he was really seeing Saturn's rings.

- He also saw sun spots, our moon's surface, and much more.

1610   **1620**   **1630**   **1640**   DEAD

1616 The Church warns Galileo not to agree with Copernicus, who believed that the earth and other planets traveled around the sun.

1632 Galileo writes a book that supports works of Copernicus and ridicules the followers of Aristotle; book gets Galileo in big trouble with the Church.

1632 Galileo is tried by the Inquisition, the court of the Church. His books are banned, and he is arrested for stating scientific truths that the Church doesn't believe in yet.

1638 Galileo publishes his final book on theories of motion and energy. He lays the groundwork for Newton to get famous with his theories of inertia.

1639 Galileo may have stared into the sun one too many times. Becomes totally blind.

1642 No more star gazing for old Galileo.

1983 Galileo is pardoned by the Roman Catholic Church. After a four-year investigation, a Church commission admits they were wrong to condemn Galileo 351 years ago.

THE TOWER TOSS

Galileo studied how objects gain speed (accelerate) as they fall and was forced to disagree with Aristotle once again. Aristotle said that since the earth is the center of the universe, it was "natural" for heavy things to fall to earth faster than light things. Of course Galileo had to test it and prove Aristotle wrong. In 1590 he demonstrated by dropping two balls of the same size but different weights off a tower. As Galileo predicted, they landed at nearly the same time.

½ lb   10 lb

HOW THE TELESCOPE WORKS

Galileo questioned everything. In college he was nicknamed the "wrangler"! What a stud!

OBJECTIVE CONVEX LENS

EYEPIECE LENS

Eye! See!

A refracting telescope has a large objective lens, which *refracts* (bends) light to form an upside-down image of a distant object. The objective lens is a convex (bulging) lens which makes things appear close to the viewer—much like a magnifying glass does. The eyepiece lens allows you to put your eye right next to the telescope and see the enlarged image.

FATHER OF THE SCIENTIFIC METHOD

The Church tried to stop Galileo, but the truth was already out. Partly because of Galileo's work with the telescope, people began to understand that making their own observations—instead of listening to authorities—was the way to find out the truth. ● Galileo's style was to develop a theory through observation and prove it through experimentation. This laid the groundwork for the scientific method and all future scientific work.

15

Name: Sir Isaac Newton
Born: December 25, 1642; Woolsthorpe, Lincolnshire, England
DEAD: March 20, 1727
Famous because: Physicist and mathematician extraordinaire. Laid the foundation of modern physics.

1664 Begins his private notebook with the line "Plato is my friend, Aristotle is my friend, but my best friend is truth."

BORN
1642

1650

1660

1642 Newton is born on Christmas day, a tiny, weak baby. He's not expected to make it through a day, much less 84 years. Born the same year Galileo died.

1644–1653 Psychotic, obsessive, insecure, and violent—possibly because he is abandoned by his mother for these 9 years while she is living with her second husband.

1661 Goes to Cambridge College. The scientific revolution is well on its way. The Dark Ages are finally starting to lighten up.

SIR ISAAC NEWTON was one of the greatest intellects of all time. He changed the world's view of mathematics, physics, optics, and astronomy. As a college student he formulated the concept of calculus and used it to understand fundamental physical phenomena. He then went on to create the reflecting telescope and explain the properties of light and color. He brought the universe into perspective with his book *Principia Mathematica*, (Mathematical Principles) in which he formulates the laws of gravity and planetary motion.

Newton was a very religious man. In trying to understand and appreciate God's creation, he came to many of his discoveries. Lucky for us that Newton was born in a time when scientific thought was more acceptable, or he might have had a fate much like Galileo's. By now the sun-centered universe theory was accepted, so Newton was able to wonder not *if* the planets moved around the sun, but how they did so.

Newton was not known for his even temperament. He was known to fly off the handle at times, and at others he'd go into complete isolation. He studied and worked with such an intensity that he would forget to eat or sleep. It was this intensity that kept him pondering concepts and solutions long after the normal person would have given up and gone home.

1665 The Apple Falls

The plague closes the university. Newton stays home and contemplates scientific phenomena, filling his secret notebook with major breakthroughs. It is during this time of isolation and deep thoughts about heavy things such as gravity that Newton watches the legendary apple fall from the tree in his mother's garden. This apparently triggers thoughts on gravity, planetary motion, and the moon's pull on the earth. This apple has come to symbolize the spark of scientific insight as well as Newton himself.

1687 Writes *Principia Mathematica*, which becomes the groundwork for the whole of modern physics and the coming of age of his three laws of motion (see next page). He develops the law of gravity, applying the word "gravitas," which is Latin for "heaviness" or "weight." This law states that every object attracts everything else around it. With the concept of gravity Newton explains the falling of apples, tides, and the orbits of the planets and comets.

1684 Edmund Halley visits Newton for help in figuring out orbits. Halley is the astronomer who would later predict the orbit of Halley's comet. (It flew by in 1985 and returns every 75 years.)

1696 Gets job making money at the London Mint. Even great thinkers have to pay the bills. As the warden, he vents some of his lifelong rage by ordering counterfeiters to be hanged.

1669 Gives birth to the understanding of calculus, a cool way to solve really hard physics problems. His secret word for it was *Fluxions*. Is appointed to a professorship at University of Cambridge.

1672 Scientist Robert Hooke, who has already done extensive work on the theory of gravity, criticizes Newton's theories on light, and Newton can't take it. He has a tantrum and goes into isolation for two years.

1671 Creates reflecting telescope. It uses mirrors to bring the stars up close and clearer than ever.

1693 Has a nervous breakdown.

1704 Newton finally publishes *Optics*, a major work on his theories of light and color. Because of his intense dislike of criticism, he has waited 30 years to publish it, until Hooke, his most verbal critic and lifelong enemy, has died.

1705 Newton is knighted and becomes Sir Isaac Newton. Receives many other honors.

1726 Gravity pulls Newton 6 feet under.

1670 | **1680** | **1690** | **1700**

DEAD

NEWTON'S THREE LAWS OF MOTION

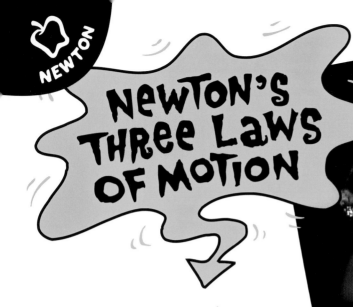

LAW 1

If something isn't moving, it won't start moving until something makes it start moving.

LAW 2

If something is moving, it won't stop moving until something makes it stop.

LAW 3

To every action there is an equal and opposite reaction.

NEWTON'S THREE LAWS CAN BE DEMONSTRATED WITH FUZZY THE CRASH DUMMY ON A SKATEBOARD:

LAW 1 Fuzzy and the skateboard are at the top of the ramp. They won't move until they are released and gravity pulls them downhill.

LAW 2 The skateboard will keep moving until something stops it, such as the wall at the bottom of the ramp. Fuzzy doesn't hit the wall and keeps moving forward.

18

"IF I HAVE SEEN FURTHER, IT IS BY STANDING ON THE SHOULDERS OF GIANTS."

This is Newton's way of acknowledging his thanks to the past scientists whose work sparked his own revelations. He was influenced by the genius of Descartes, Copernicus, Galileo, Archimedies, Kepler, and others. (Any of these dead guys sound familiar?)

I don't know about that gravity stuff, but he sure makes a great fig cookie.

LAW 3

The skateboard hits the wall (that's the action). The wall pushes back on the skateboard, and it goes back up the ramp (that's the reaction).

Name: Benjamin Franklin
Born: January 17, 1706; Boston, Massachusetts
DEAD: April 17, 1790
Famous because: Flew kite in an electric storm

1718 Printer's apprentice for brother James. Writes political humor under the fake name of "Silence Dogood" so his brother will print it.

BORN
1706

1710

1720

Fifteenth child born to the Franklin family. Those Bostonians know how to live.

1729 Acquires *Pennsylvania Gazette*. Marries Deborah Read (any coincidence in buying a newspaper company and marrying someone named "read"?).

Ben Franklin: Man of Many Talents

Ben Franklin was a world-famous printer, publisher, philosopher, politician, educator, author, general, diplomat, and inventor—as well as a scientist! He played a major role in the cultural, political, and scientific formulation of the newborn United States. And he was a real character with a great sense of humor, cleverly sharing his wit and playful sarcasm in *Poor Richard's Almanack*. After publishing the first issue in 1732, Franklin quickly became the most widely read and quoted author in the American colonies.

As a politician, Franklin served as a colonial ambassador to Great Britain until the American Revolution in 1776. During the war he was part of the Second Constitutional Convention and brought France and the United States together as allies (friends), and helped draft the Declaration of Independence.

Ben retired at age 42 to pursue his passion for scientific research. He started and was president of the American Philosophical Society, the first society devoted to science. He questioned everything, yet focused his efforts on practical things. The Franklin stove, for example, arose from his desire to get rid of chimney smoke. He devised a whale oil candle, which gave off a clearer, whiter light. His ability to organize information, simplify theories, and use his findings to improve the quality of life are best depicted by his well-known electricity experiments.

Franklin—everyone knows his name, everyone loved him, but he's dead now.

June 1752:
Franklin Flies Silk Kite in Thunderstorm

Franklin showed that lightning and electricity are the same thing. He built a kite out of silk scarves and a pair of crossed sticks. He tied a metal rod to the top of the kite, and attached a key and a silk ribbon at the end of the string. When a storm approached and dark clouds appeared, Franklin and his 22-year-old son boldly flew the kite. Despite what the history books may say, Franklin's kite was never struck by lightning. The electricity in the passing clouds flowed down the kite string. When Franklin touched his knuckle to the key, he got an electric spark!

1730   **1740**   **1750**   **1770**   **1780**   **DEAD**

1742-44 Invents Franklin stove.

1749 Heavy into experimenting with electricity, Franklin uses electricity to zap a turkey and to light the fire to cook the bird.

1751 *Experiments and Observations on Electricity* is published in London; Franklin founds Pennsylvania Hospital and is elected to Pennsylvania Assembly.

1750 Franklin gets zapped by his own lightning-rod experiment, clarifying the relationship between lightning and electricity.

1753 Appointed deputy postmaster general. Helps General Edward Braddock defend Pennsylvania against Indian attacks.

1776 Signs Declaration of Independence on July 4.

1790 Franklin short circuits. No spark left in old Ben. Flies the big kite in the sky.

Lightning Rods Control the Zap

Lightning rods decrease the chance of your house getting struck by lightning. Clouds are charged with static electricity. A thunderstorm creates a strong negative charge (–) along the bottom of clouds. The top of the clouds become positively charged (+). The negative charge on the bottom of the clouds causes a strong positive charge on the ground below.

When the charge in the clouds is strong enough, it forces a path to the ground through the air and discharges a flash of lightning. Franklin's lightning rod (like those used today) had a wire that connected the rod to the ground. If lightning strikes, the electricity follows the path down the lightning rod and travels harmlessly along the wire to the ground.

FRANKLIN

1 Electrons have a negative charge, shown like this –

2 Opposites attract
– +
– +
– +

3 Like charges *repel*—push away from—each other.

+ + ←→ + +
+   +

Franklin says, "Early to bed and early to rise, makes a man healthy, wealthy, and wise."

The Franklin bifocals—another example of necessity being the mother of invention.

TATIC ELECTRICITY

Rub a blown-up balloon in your hair and stick it on the wall. When your hair rubs against the balloon, electrons (–) from your hair are rubbed off onto the balloon giving the balloon a negative charge. When the negatively charged balloon approaches the wall, other negative charges in the wall are repelled and move farther away, leaving a positive charge at the spot where the balloon touches the wall. That's why the balloon sticks to the wall.

OTHER FRANKLIN INVENTIONS

• swim fins

• glass harmonica

• Franklin stove

• a chair that converts into a ladder

• librarian pole to get books off tall shelves

23

Name: The Montgolfier Brothers
Jacques-Etienne Montgolfier
  Born: August 26, 1745; Annonay, France
  DEAD: August 2, 1799
Joseph-Michel Montgolfier
  Born: January 6, 1740; Annonay, France
  DEAD: June 26, 1810
Famous because: They invented the hot-air balloon.

1772 Daddy retires and an older brother dies, leaving Etienne to manage the family business. He brings it to new heights with his innovative ideas and experiments. The shining star does it again.

BORN

1750

1760

1740 Joseph born.

1745 Etienne born.

1777 Ben Franklin moves to Paris. As a scientist and inventor, Franklin is very excited about the idea of hot-air balloons and offers support and advice to both the Montgolfiers and their rival, Jacques Charles to keep their competition healthy and progressive.

The Montgolfier (mont-GULF-ee-ay) brothers were two of the sixteen children born to a wealthy eighteenth-century French paper manufacturer. Joseph-Michel (who went by the name of Joseph) was an absentminded, mostly self-educated dreamer. He ran away in his teens, later tried to be a farmer, didn't make it in school, tried and failed in business. He was pretty much a loser. Joseph was deeply in debt and well on his way to becoming the black sheep of the family when he came up with this balloon idea.

Jacques-Etienne (called Etienne—AY-tee-ann—which is French for Stephen), on the other hand, was the shining star of the Montgolfier family. Early in life he showed talent in both chemical and mechanical experimentation. He became an architect, which gave him the formal background in science and technology he'd need later on for their balloon escapades. Etienne also had influential friends in Paris who helped the Montgolfiers get their balloon career off the ground.

1783: Ballooning gets off the ground.
Hydrogen, a gas lighter than air had just been discovered. The Montgolfier brothers thought this "inflammable air," came from the fire. They built a cloth globe, 35 feet in diameter, and launched it from a big fire in the town square. It flew for about ten minutes and landed. Next, they launched a balloon with the first aeronauts—a sheep, a duck, and a rooster! Copying the experiment, physicists Jacques Charles and Jean and Nicolas Robert built a leak-proof hydrogen balloon. It landed nearby in Gonesse. Baffled, the town peasants stabbed the "monster" with pitchforks before it could do them in.
The Montgolfiers' balloon was filled with hot air, not hydrogen. This misunderstanding led to two different techniques of ballooning; hot air balloons, and hydrogen and helium balloons.

1784 The big balloon goes up. It's 102 feet in diameter and 126 feet high. It holds six people, water buckets, fuel, and a wood stove for hot air. The fabric splits, the basket falls. This is Joseph's first and only trip; Etienne (the chicken) never makes a flight. Maybe they have the right idea—send others up in their balloons while they safely watch from the ground.

1770   1780   1790   **DEAD 1799**   1800   **DEAD 1810**

1783 Joseph is named a member of the Academy of Sciences. Etienne is a corresponding member of the National Institute. They both use their clout to save lives during the French Revolution, when the common people rise up against the aristocracy and many people are beheaded.

1784 Balloon mania hits France by way of dress designers, toy makers, interior decorators . . . everything is balloons!! If it were 200 years later, balloon video games would be the rage.

1792 Joseph invents a new kind of water pump. Not as exciting as a balloon, but it shows that he had more than one good idea in his life.

1785 Jean-François Rozier (a fellow balloonist) plans to cross the English channel in a combination hydrogen-and-hot-air balloon. Ben Franklin tries to warn him and others that technology hasn't caught up to such a grandiose experiment. Rozier does the big "crash and burn." Guess he doesn't know you can't mix flames and a flammable gas such as hydrogen—kaboom!

1799 Etienne dead. Up, up, and away. . . forever.

1801 Joseph hired as instructor and administrator of Conservatory of Arts and Industry. For a dropout he ends up doing pretty well for himself.

1810 Joseph dead. Makes his last ascent and keeps on going.

Up, Up, and Away

Hot-air balloons work on the basic principle that hot air rises and cold air falls. Depending on its temperature, the same amount of air takes up more or less space. As air heats up, the air molecules become more active and move away from each other. Cold air molecules are slower and huddle together. And because air has weight, a lot of cold air packed into a balloon is heavier than less hot air dancing around in that same balloon.

The hot air in the balloon weighs less than the air around it, so the balloon goes up, just like a bubble in water or bubbles in a glass of soda pop.

DENSITY This business of cold air molecules huddling together is called *density*. Cold air is more dense, or more tightly packed together, than hot air. Population density describes how many people are living in a space.

For example, an apartment building is more densely populated than a residential home. Let's see how this affects a balloon:

Burners

Basket

THE ASCENT

The balloon itself is called the envelope, and it holds the hot air. A gas burner in the wicker basket heats the air in the balloon to about 212° F (or 100°C). As the air heats up, the air molecules start dancing around a lot more, taking up more space. About 25% of the air leaves out of the bottom of the balloon. The balloon now weighs less, and is carried upward.

THE DESCENT

To get the balloon to descend, or go down, the burner is shut off. As the air cools, it contracts, or squeezes together, making room for more air to enter the bottom of the balloon. The air in the balloon becomes more dense, the weight of the balloon increases and it comes down (you hope!) slowly.

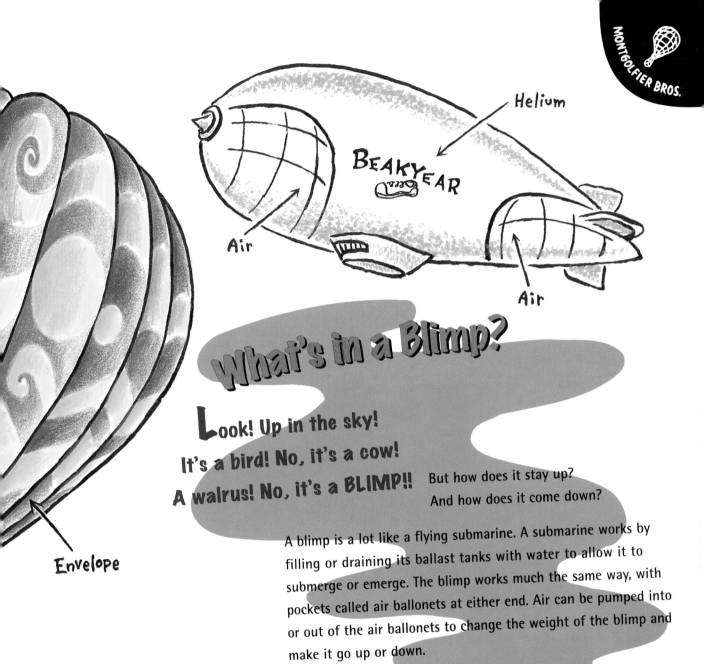

Helium

BEAKYEAR

Air

Air

Envelope

What's in a Blimp?

Look! Up in the sky!
It's a bird! No, it's a cow!
A walrus! No, it's a BLIMP!!
But how does it stay up?
And how does it come down?

A blimp is a lot like a flying submarine. A submarine works by filling or draining its ballast tanks with water to allow it to submerge or emerge. The blimp works much the same way, with pockets called air ballonets at either end. Air can be pumped into or out of the air ballonets to change the weight of the blimp and make it go up or down.

The main body of the blimp is filled with helium, a gas that is seven times less dense than air and is non-flammable. A balloon full of helium (like a birthday balloon) will take off because it is lighter than air.

Also, a blimp sometimes has lightbulbs arranged in an attractive corporate logo.

It could be a very "uplifting" experience if I filled this rat suit with helium.

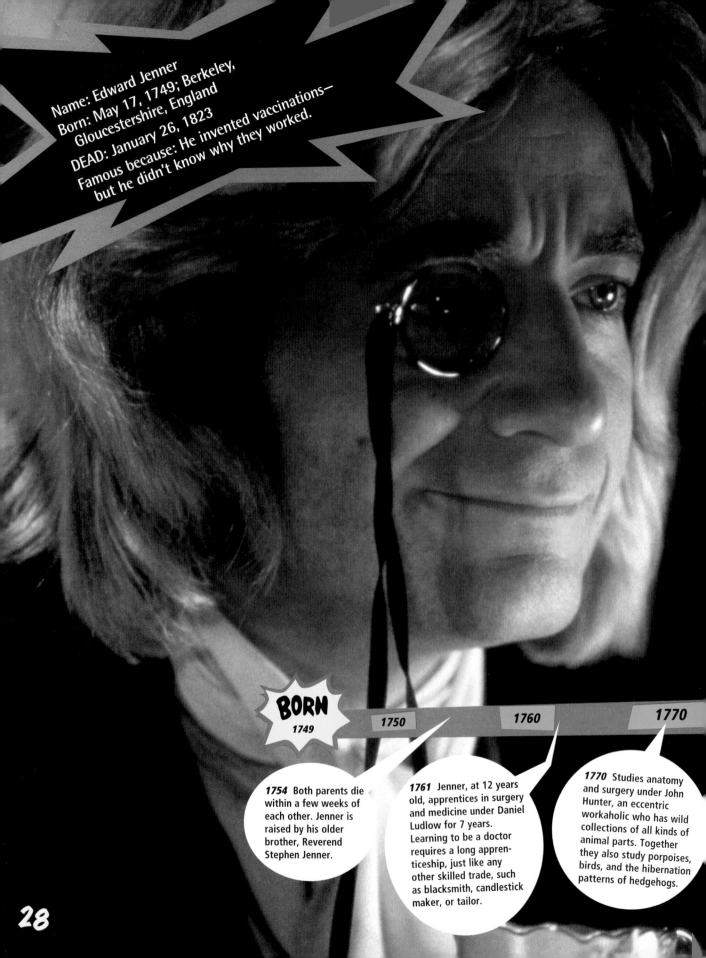

Name: Edward Jenner
Born: May 17, 1749; Berkeley,
Gloucestershire, England
DEAD: January 26, 1823
Famous because: He invented vaccinations—
but he didn't know why they worked.

BORN
1749

1750

1760

1770

1754 Both parents die within a few weeks of each other. Jenner is raised by his older brother, Reverend Stephen Jenner.

1761 Jenner, at 12 years old, apprentices in surgery and medicine under Daniel Ludlow for 7 years. Learning to be a doctor requires a long apprenticeship, just like any other skilled trade, such as blacksmith, candlestick maker, or tailor.

1770 Studies anatomy and surgery under John Hunter, an eccentric workaholic who has wild collections of all kinds of animal parts. Together they also study porpoises, birds, and the hibernation patterns of hedgehogs.

Edward Jenner's father was a clergyman with the Church of England, and so he was born among the upper crust. He did things that wealthy kids did—such as ride and hunt—and he also learned to read and write Latin and Greek. The discipline at the private boys' school he attended was pretty straightforward. There were various size canes to suit each crime—you break a rule, you get your butt whacked. Jenner was good at steering clear of trouble. Unlike most of his schoolmates, Jenner was into the natural sciences. He had several hibernating mice and a great collection of fossils.

THE COWPOX STORY

Back in Jenner's time, thousands of people were dying of a horrible disease called smallpox. A pox is a skin eruption, and many viruses—chicken pox, smallpox, measles, German measles—cause them. Jenner noticed that the only people spared from smallpox were those who milked cows. Instead, they got cowpox, a disease like smallpox but much milder, from touching lesions (sores) on the teats and udders of cows. Jenner got the idea that catching cowpox somehow protected these people from catching smallpox. He wondered if he gave someone cowpox on purpose, they too would be protected.

To test his theory, Jenner decided to actually draw pus out of a cowpox sore with a needle and inject it into a perfectly healthy person. (We're talking really gross stuff here.) In 1796 Jenner injected 8-year-old James Phipps with a bit of cowpox pus he got from a milkmaid named Sarah Nelmes. The boy got a mild case of cowpox. Two months later, Jenner injected James with fresh smallpox pus, and he didn't get sick! By giving James cowpox, Jenner had made the boy immune to smallpox. He was now permanently protected.

MEDICINE OF THE DARK AGES

Before Jenner and the cowpox idea, plagues, scarlet fever, typhoid, cholera, and other killer diseases were a way of life (or death). Disease preventions included exorcisms (driving out demons), wearing garlic, using oils, and bloodletting (cutting open the vein to let the bad blood out). Jenner started a whole new wave of medical science. However, he never knew that smallpox was caused by a virus, a very small microscopic organism. He also didn't know that cowpox pus stimulated the body to produce antibodies, which fought the smallpox virus.

Today, we still get inoculations to protect ourselves from viruses. However, we use inoculates grown under sterile laboratory conditions instead of cow pus.

DEAD

SCORE

GERMS 1
JENNER 0

1780

1790

1800

1773 Practices medicine. Protects many people against smallpox with pus from other people's smallpox sores. The healthy folks get a mild case of smallpox but then are immune to a fatal (deadly) case of the disease. It's a dangerous practice— sometimes a little bit can kill you.

1786 Makes obscure natural history findings, such as the unusual nesting behavior of cuckoos. When hatched in a sparrow's nest, a cuckoo dumps sparrow eggs out of the sparrow's own nest. Writes a paper that should have been titled "Murder in the Sparrow Nest."

1778 Jenner gets dumped by his wealthy fiancée. After a 10-year recovery period, he marries Katherine Kingscote and moves to Chantry Cottage in his hometown of Berkeley, England.

1789 Falsely believes that cowpox comes from a disease on horses' feet. When you are experimenting, you have to try everything.

1790 Jenner *inoculates* (or injects) his own one-year-old son with pus from a swinepox sore. The kid develops some pus spots, but nothing serious. A little later, he gives his son some smallpox and nothing happens. So far so good! Two years later gives him more smallpox matter—still nothing! Another inoculation success story.

1798 Smallpox doesn't just disappear overnight. Many doctors are skeptical of Jenner's findings. In truth, some doctors aren't giving the vaccine correctly and some are using the wrong stuff from the cows, but it still makes Jenner look bad.

1823 Jenner's not immune to everything.

THE GERMS

You get an infection when a germ, either a virus or a bacteria, invades your body. Both kinds of germs can only be seen with a very powerful microscope. Viruses are much smaller than bacteria.

BACTERIA

Diseases caused by bacteria:
strep throat
earache
pinkeye

HUMAN CELL

VIRUSES

Diseases caused by viruses:
colds   chicken pox
measles   mumps
whooping cough
polio   AIDS

AIDS

(Acquired Immune Deficiency Syndrome) is one of the most infamous viruses present today. AIDS weakens the immune system itself—the very weapon the body needs to fight off disease. Scientists are working very hard to find a vaccine and a cure for AIDS. The good news is that it's really hard to get AIDS. You can't get it through mosquito bites. You can't get it from a sneeze. And most importantly, you can't get it from hugging someone who has AIDS.

VIRUS ATTACK!

Viruses are teeny tiny things that make people and other living creatures sick. Here's how they do it:

1 A virus locks onto a cell (the little things your body is made of).

2 The virus drills a hole into the cell and dumps its protein inside.

3 The virus multiplies inside your cell and takes it over.

4 The cell bursts open, releasing lots of viruses to go attack lots more cells.

Your Immune System Fights Infection

1 The first line of defense: Your skin

Germs see cuts and scrapes as a ticket into your body. Your skin blocks germs and keeps them out, so keep open wounds clean and germ-free.

2 The second line of defense: White blood cells

White blood cells are always on patrol looking for germs, and when they find them, they eat 'em. They can eat about 100 germs each before being carried out by snot, phlegm, or pus— your body's trash.

3 Third line of defense: Antibodies

Antibodies fight off germs they've seen before. You probably got vaccinated against German measles, tetanus, influenza, diphtheria, whooping cough, polio, and more when you were a baby. The antibodies against those viruses and bacteria are still in your bloodstream ready to fight if attacked.

skin

white blood cells

antibodies

JENNER

GERMS WELCOME

This is udder-ly disgusting!

SMALLPOX IS WIPED OUT!
The vaccine worked!

Smallpox doesn't exist today. The last person who had it was in Somalia in 1977. Since everyone else was vaccinated, there was no one left to give it to—so it died out. Smallpox vaccines aren't given any more because there is no more risk of getting the disease. Most adults (but not all) have a dime-size scar at the top of their arm from a smallpox vaccination— a little needle prick full of smallpox virus. Go check out the smallpox vaccine mark on your parents, your grandparents, or some other adult.

Name: Maria Mitchell
Born: August 1, 1818; Nantucket, Massachusetts
DEAD: June 28, 1889
Famous because: America's first professional female astronomer. Found Mitchell's Comet.

BORN
1818

1830

1836 Becomes first librarian at the Nantucket Atheneum (ah-tha-NAY-um)—the town library. Holds position for 20 years. Teaches herself two foreign languages and advanced mathematics.

1831 Counts the seconds of solar eclipse with her dad. (He's the astronomer who instilled in her a love of science.)

1832 Sea captains trust 14-year-old Mitchell to set their nautical clocks for long whaling voyages.

1835 Starts her own school for girls.

Maria (that's pronounced mah-RYE-ah) Mitchell was a talented astronomer dedicated to encouraging girls to study science and mathematics. In Mitchell's day, girls didn't have the privilege of a college education, but her parents made sure all their children were well educated and raised them to be independent and self sufficient. At age 17, Mitchell started her own school for girls and at 18 she was Nantucket's first librarian.

The discovery of Mitchell's Comet led her to receive many honors and awards—many of them a first for a woman—including election to the American Academy of Arts and Sciences and the American Association for the Advancement of Science. In addition she was chosen to work on the United States Nautical Almanac. She was the first professor of astronomy at Vassar College (a women's college), and was president of the Association for the Advancement of Women.

When Mitchell died, her sister crossed out all the personal information in her journals, so we know very little about her personal life. Her family, friends, and pupils from Vassar established the Maria Mitchell Association to preserve her birthplace and to continue her work in astronomy and science education. It's in Nantucket, Massachusetts. Go check it out.

October 1, 1847 at 10:30 P.M.

Mitchell's Comet Discovered

Mitchell discovered a telescopic comet, one that is not visible with the naked eye. During her parents' dinner party that night, Mitchell slipped up to the roof of the Pacific National Bank, the building in which her family lived in Nantucket. Through her Dollond telescope, one of the best telescopes of the day, she noticed a foreign object in the sky that was 5 degrees above Polaris (the North Star) and plotted its course. The King of Denmark had offered a gold medal in 1831 for the discovery of a telescopic comet. Mitchell wasn't racing for a medal, but she did see her comet days before other people in Europe who tried to make claim to it. On March 30, 1849, Mitchell became the first American and the first woman to receive an award of this kind.

DEAD

1840	1850	1860	1870

1843 Drifts from the Quakers because her mind is "not settled on religious subjects." Enjoys intellectual freedom of the Unitarian Church.

1848 Hired by United States Nautical Almanac for $300 per year to calculate whereabouts of Venus and collect other astronomical data. Holds position for 19 years, making her the first professional female astronomer.

1865 Becomes America's first female professor of astronomy when Vassar College opens. Retires in 1888.

1875–1876 President of the American Association for the Advancement of Women.

1889 Maria plots her final course. The stars fade for Maria.

THE COMET ~ A DIRTY SNOWBALL

A comet is a lot of frozen gases and debris, much like a dirty snowball. Just past Pluto's orbit are big chunks of ice, possibly left over from the formation of our Solar System. A comet is one such ice chunk that has gotten knocked into our solar system and hurtles toward the sun.

Let's see what's in a comet.

Main Ingredients:

One **BIG** chunk of ice
Ammonia
Carbon Dioxide
Nitrogen
Dirt
Miscellaneous space junk

Add Later:

Heat
Solar winds

PARTS OF A COMET

The **nucleus** is the solid, frozen chunk of junk we just assembled. It can be several miles in diameter. A comet spends most of its life as the dirty snowball we call the nucleus and only begins to change when it approaches the sun.

The **coma**, which can be several hundred miles wide, is made of particles of dust mixed with gases that boil off the nucleus as the comet gets closer to the heat of the sun.

The **tail** forms when the coma is blown back by solar winds. If a comet is traveling away from the sun, it travels tail first.

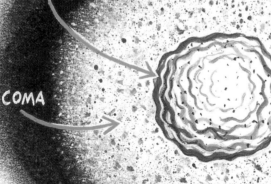

NUCLEUS

COMA

TAIL

A comet doesn't give off its own light, but we can see it because it **reflects**, or bounces back off, the light of the sun. Sunlight also reflects, or bounces off, the moon and other planets otherwise we wouldn't be able to see them.

Shooting stars are actually **meteors**, pieces of rock that hit the earth's atmosphere at over 100,000 mph. They don't glow from reflected light, but from the friction of hitting the earth's atmosphere at such high speeds.

itchell's Comet has a hyperbolic, or open-ended, path. It passed through our solar system once and left, never to return again.

Many comets, however, travel in an elliptical orbit around the sun—like the planets do—and have predictable schedules. Halley's Comet, for example, is on an orbit that takes 75 years to complete. It passed by the earth in 1910 and 1985 and will return again in 2060. How old will you be in 2060?

I don't need a telescope to see that there's a RAT attached to this comet.

MITCHELL'S THOUGHTS

ON SCIENCE

"We especially need imagination in science. It is not all mathematics, nor all logic, but it is somewhat beauty and poetry."

"We see most when we are most determined to see."

ON WOMEN

"When I see a woman sew, I think of science. When she puts an exquisite fine needle exactly the same distance from the last stitch as that stands from the one before, I think what capacity she has for using a micrometer!" (A micrometer is a scientific measuring instrument.)

ON EDUCATION

"I think, as a general rule, that teachers talk too much."

Name: Thomas Alva Edison
Born: February 11, 1847; Milan, Ohio
DEAD: October 18, 1931
Famous because: Made light bulb user-friendly.
Invented the phonograph and the movie camera,
among other things. Held 1,093 patents.

1854 At age 8, teacher thinks
Edison is a dunce and a misfit.
Edison refuses to go to school. Mom
teaches him at home. Does every
physics experiment in *Natural and
Experimental Philosophy*.

BORN
1847

1850

1860

1853 Experiments with fire. Burns
down the family barn. Young Edison
attempts human balloon by coaxing a
friend to drink baking soda and other
powders to inflate him with gas to
make the friend lighter than air.
Friend gets sick. Edison gets spanked.

1862 Edison saves stationmaster's
3-year-old son from being flattened
by a rolling boxcar. In gratitude,
stationmaster teaches Edison to
operate the telegraph—the beginning
of Edison's electronics career.

Thomas Alva Edison was the most prolific inventor in history. With 1,093 patents to his credit, his innovations, ambitions, and inventions changed the course of human events, going far beyond the inventions he is best known for—the phonograph and the incandescent light. His work not only made electric light and power possible, but also brought about the recording and motion picture industries. Driven by his passion for invention, Edison wanted to out-invent everybody else. He declared himself a "commercial inventor" and consciously geared his focus to things that satisfy real needs and increase the convenience and pleasure of the people who use them.

To this day, Edison is truly an inspiration for innovators. He showed us that with persistence and a willingness to try all the options (or at least, if there's the possibility of making some money), one can create the seemingly impossible. When asked if he thought himself a genius he replied, "genius is ninety-nine percent perspiration and one percent inspiration."

1876
The Wizard of Menlo Park

At age 29, Edison built the world's first all-purpose research lab that was designed solely to be an invention factory. He promised to turn out a minor invention every ten days and a "big trick" every six months. Edison had hand-selected a team of specialists to help him turn his ideas into realities, and before long he had 40 different projects going at the same time and was applying for as many as 400 patents a year. Menlo Park was the first industrial research laboratory and was imitated 20 years later by giant corporations in both Europe and America.

1877 Edison completes the phonograph and beats Bell to the punch. Using a tinfoil cylinder as his first record, Edison records "Mary Had a Little Lamb".

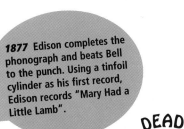

DEAD

1870   1880   1890

1869 Receives first patent for an electric vote recorder, a device that quickly displays legislators' votes. Politicians don't want it. Edison decides to invent only the things that people want.

1871 Edison takes a day off on Christmas Day to marry 15-year-old Mary Stilwell. They eventually have three kids; two of whom are nicknamed for the Morse code signals "Dot" and "Dash".

1879 After hundreds of trials and experiments, Edison invents an inexpensive, long-lasting light bulb.

1889 In a darkened room, Edison projects images onto a screen of a man walking about and tipping his hat. It's the first practical motion-picture camera and the movie industry is born.

1931 Edison flips his last switch. Lights out for old Tom.

HOW A LIGHT BULB WORKS

EDISON LIGHTS UP YOUR LIFE

Electricity is the flow of electrons through an unbroken loop called a *circuit*. When a light bulb is screwed into a socket and the switch is turned on, the electrical circuit is completed. Current flows through the *filament*.

Electrons flow smoothly until their path narrows at the filament. When the path narrows, *resistance* is created and electrons start bumping and rubbing up against each other, trying to go forward. When electricity meets resistance, it has to work harder to move through the wire, which causes the wire in the bulb to heat up to 5,500 degrees Fahrenheit and glow.

Edison knew that the key to making a light bulb work was to find a metal that wouldn't burn out when it heated up. Certain metals will combine with oxygen in the air and burn. Edison experimented with several combinations of metals and gasses to come up with a filament that wouldn't melt or burn up when it got hot. He ended up using a carbon filament in a vacuum tube (where all the air has been sucked out).

FILAMENT

GAS

GLASS BULB

GLASS ROD

Today's light bulb is made with a tungsten filament that is wound in a tight coil and a gas called *argon*. Argon gas in the bulb doesn't combine with tungsten, so the metal is not destroyed.

Birth of the Music Industry
The Phonograph

Edison was the first to record sound and play it back. He was the president of the North American Recording Company and decided who and what got recorded. He recorded works of great composers such as Strauss, Gounod, Mendelssohn, and Chopin.

Edison's phonograph led to the multi-billion dollar recording and music industry we know today. If Edison only knew that he helped Metallica.

Other Edison Stuff:

✳ The light bulb would be useless without support, so Edison worked on lamps, electrical generators, central stations, distribution lines, meters, fuses, plugs, switches, and more.

✳ He improved Bell's telephone with a carbon transmitter, which let voice be heard much more clearly.

✳ He made an electric powered, revolving typewriter wheel. It was perfected 100 years later in the IBM Selectric.

Good ideas used to look like this.

39

Name: Alexander Graham Bell
Born: March 3, 1847; Edinburgh, Scotland
DEAD: August 2, 1922
Famous because: Invented the telephone.

1872 Opens a school for teachers of the deaf in Boston, Massachusetts. Bell gets financial backing from Gardiner Hubbard, a patent attorney specializing in mechanical and electrical inventions.

BORN 1847

1855

1865

1862 At age fifteen, Bell drops out of Royal High School to study speech with his grandfather in London.

1874 Bell meets Mr. Watson, who becomes his faithful assistant. Watson has been experimenting with exploding torpedoes. (Good thing they didn't try to make an exploding telephone.)

Alexander Graham Bell was quite the curious guy. He not only invented the telephone—his most notable claim to fame—but he also invented or helped develop the hydrofoil boat, the phonograph, air conditioning, and many other items. He made a human-carrying kite and a very crude airplane, but the Wright brothers beat him to the punch on that one. He taught deaf people how to speak and studied how sounds are emitted by vibrating objects, such as your vocal cords and tuning forks. He used the idea of vibrating frequencies in the human voice as the springboard for sending voice signals as electricity over wires. The result was the telephone.

March 10, 1876:

"Mr. Watson, come here, I want you."

After countless weeks of experimenting with wires and sound, Bell and his assistant, Mr. Watson, were experimenting with battery acid and other chemicals. Bell spilled battery acid on his pants and needed assistance quickly. "Mr. Watson, come here, I want you," he said. Watson, who was well out of earshot, heard every word clearly. These became the first words spoken over the telephone. (Being a speech teacher, you'd think he could have come up with something more clever.)

The fight was on. A big legal dispute arose between Bell and Western Union Telegraph Company over the rights to the telephone. At least 10 inventors claimed major parts and 600 inventors claimed minor parts of the telephone as their own invention, and Western Union controlled the patents of the main inventors. To avoid endless court costs, the two came to an agreement. Western Union transferred its telephone patents to the Bell Telephone Company, and Bell gave Western Union percentages of stock.

So maybe Bell didn't think up every little working detail of the telephone, but he was undisputedly the first to make the whole thing actually work.

DEAD

Timeline

375 | **1885** | **1895** | **1905** | **1915**

1876 Invents the telephone.

1877 Bell marries Mabel Hubbard, Gardiner's daughter, who is ten years younger. Mabel is a deaf student whom he has taught to talk (it's hard for deaf people to talk, since they can't hear what words should sound like). On his wedding day, Bell weighs in at 165 pounds.

1878 After a year of Mabel's cooking, Bell porks out to 214 pounds. He eventually gets up to 250 pounds and stays there.

1881–1885 Creates wax phonograph, which improves on the recording sound of Edison's tinfoil phonograph. Bell is bummed, however, that the original invention slipped through his fingers.

1887 Meets six-year-old Helen Keller, who is both blind and deaf. Befriends and helps her throughout her life to improve her communication.

1908 Bell begins experimenting with hydrofoil boats. The lift produced by water moving past the foils (the metal sheets on the boat's bottom) raises the hull clear out of the water, and the boat "flies" on the foils.

1919 Bell's Hydrofoil HD-4 sets speed record of 70.86 miles per hour. It is too radical for military use, but holds speed record for ten years.

1947 Bell's line gets disconnected. He's really dead!!

41

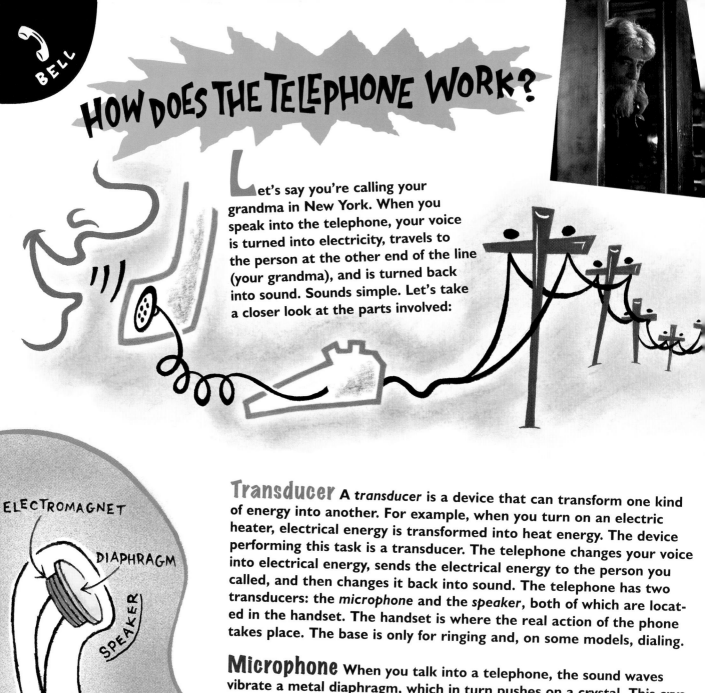

HOW DOES THE TELEPHONE WORK?

Let's say you're calling your grandma in New York. When you speak into the telephone, your voice is turned into electricity, travels to the person at the other end of the line (your grandma), and is turned back into sound. Sounds simple. Let's take a closer look at the parts involved:

Transducer

A *transducer* is a device that can transform one kind of energy into another. For example, when you turn on an electric heater, electrical energy is transformed into heat energy. The device performing this task is a transducer. The telephone changes your voice into electrical energy, sends the electrical energy to the person you called, and then changes it back into sound. The telephone has two transducers: the *microphone* and the *speaker*, both of which are located in the handset. The handset is where the real action of the phone takes place. The base is only for ringing and, on some models, dialing.

Microphone

When you talk into a telephone, the sound waves vibrate a metal diaphragm, which in turn pushes on a crystal. This crystal produces electrical impulses each time it is squeezed. Your sound waves have been converted into electrical energy, which travels along phone lines at nearly the speed of light (186,000 miles per second). The electricity goes to an *exchange* where operators or computers connect it to grandma's house.

Speaker

When grandma picks up the phone, the electrical signals pass through a transducer called an *electromagnet*. Its magnetism gets stronger and weaker based on the strength of the electrical signals. The magnetism makes a speaker cone vibrate, producing sound waves that grandma hears as your voice, right in her ear.

The invention of the telephone led to the development of the hearing aid. A hearing aid amplifies sound, which means it makes noises sound louder. Before the hearing aid, people used to hold a horn or megaphone up to their ear to catch sound waves. Hold your hand cupped behind your ear. Can you hear things louder?

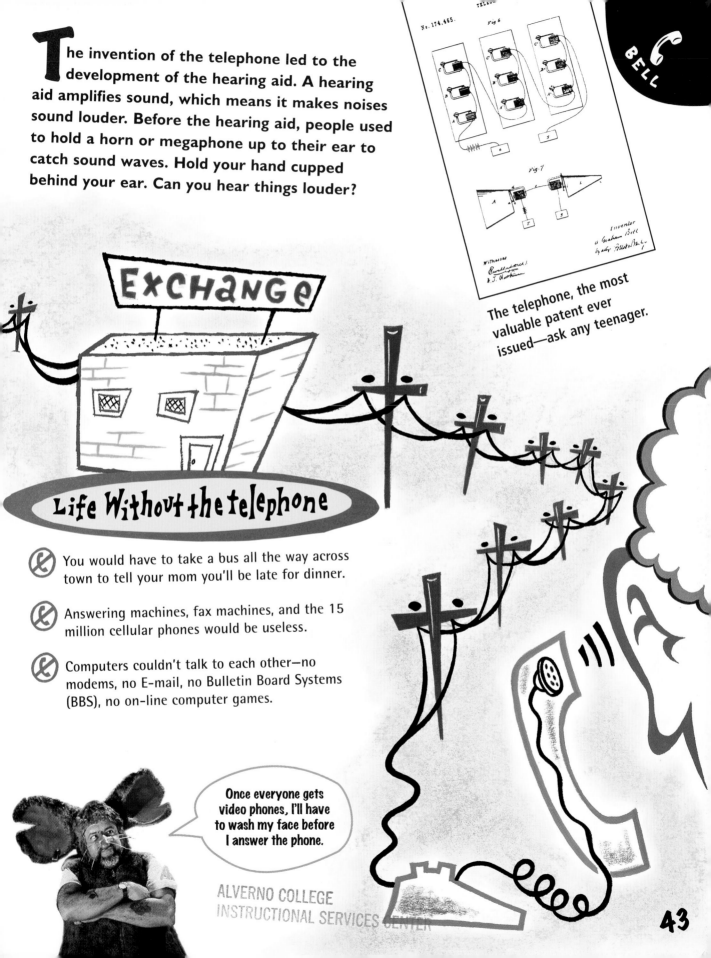

No. 174,465.

BELL

The telephone, the most valuable patent ever issued—ask any teenager.

EXCHANGE

Life Without the telephone

🚫 You would have to take a bus all the way across town to tell your mom you'll be late for dinner.

🚫 Answering machines, fax machines, and the 15 million cellular phones would be useless.

🚫 Computers couldn't talk to each other—no modems, no E-mail, no Bulletin Board Systems (BBS), no on-line computer games.

Once everyone gets video phones, I'll have to wash my face before I answer the phone.

Name: Marie Curie, born Manya Sklodowska (now there's a mouthful)
Born: November 7, 1867; Warsaw, Poland
DEAD: July 4, 1934
Famous because: She discovered the elements polonium and radium and won two Nobel prizes for her work in radioactivity and isolating those two elements.

1895–1896 Wilhelm Roentgen discovers that X-rays pass through opaque substances. As a result, Henri Becquerel finds that uranium sends out rays of light energy strong enough to expose photographic paper. Curie does her doctoral work on the source of these rays.

1890 Leaves Poland for Paris. Poland is occupied by Russia, so it is very oppressive. Polish students are forced to speak Russian and women can't go to the university.

1896 First daughter, Irene, born.

BORN
1867

1880

1890

1891 A devoted student at the Sorbonne in Paris, Curie lives on bread, butter, and tea. She lives in the coldest, cheapest places, but is dedicated to her scientific research.

1893 Becomes first woman to receive degree in physics from the Sorbonne—and she's number one in her class.

1895 Marie and Pierre tie the knot. They are aglow with happiness. Marie wears a navy blue wool suit—something practical she can wear in the lab after the wedding.

1884 At age 16, Curie graduates first in her class with prizes for excellence in mathematics, history, Russian literature, French, German, and English.

Marie Curie is well-known for her dedicated work in physics and chemistry which led to the discoveries of the radioactive elements polonium and radium and two Nobel prizes. Her family was such an important part of her work that often when you study Marie Curie, you learn about the whole glow-in-the-dark clan. Her husband Pierre worked with her in the lab to uncover the secrets of radiation. Her daughter Irene went on to win her own Nobel prize for chemistry.

As a girl, Curie was a bright, shy, and introspective student from a competitive Polish family. Her dad was a dedicated physics and mathematics professor, not a super-excitable kind of guy, who kept a stone face through life's extreme highs and lows. As a result, Curie grew up to be hard working and self-driven and didn't let life's tragedies or fame get in the way of her research. Einstein said she was "the only person fame has not corrupted."

With the attitude of pure scientists, Marie and Pierre Curie never made a profit from radium—and they certainly could have. Instead, they published their methods and findings with the hope of aiding their fellow humans. To honor their many contributions the "curie" has been named as a measure of radioactivity.

1898–1902
Curies isolate polonium and radium

In a drafty, cold, dark lab, Marie and Pierre work to isolate radioactive elements from a ton of pitchblende, a radioactive pile of tar which contains the elements uranium and thorium. However, the Curies know there's something else in there, because the pile registers over four times the radioactivity of uranium and thorium.

Curie performs test after test to isolate these mysterious elements. It's like looking for a needle in a haystack. Finally, she discovers polonium and radium, each a whole new element.

Curie's main scientific contribution is the concept of *radioactivity*, a word she coined from the Latin word for ray *(radius)*. This makes thorium, uranium, polonium, and radium *radioelements*, or elements of the periodic table that emit radiation.

THE ATOMIC AGE DAWNS

Everyone is talking about tiny particles called atoms, which are so small that way more than a million of them would fit in a grain of sand. Each element is a different atom. Curie showed that the atom is an ever-changing, unstable miniature solar system full of many particles and forces, instead of being a solid unit of matter. It is neither indestructable nor indivisible. This little concept leads to, among other things, theories on cancer causes and cures, nuclear bombs, and nuclear power.

1904 Pierre and Becquerel test effects of radioactivity on mice and guinea pigs. They find that radium gas changes blood and lung tissue and lowers one's ability to fight diseases. Unfortunately, they don't make the connection that it does the same to humans. So they all continue to touch, breath in, and expose themselves to radioactivity. To this day, Curie's notebooks contain lethal doses of radioactive contamination.

1911 Curie awarded Nobel prize in chemistry for the discovery of polonium (named for her homeland of Poland) and the isolation of radium, the most powerful radioactive substance that exists in nature.

DEAD

1900   1910   1920   1930

1903 The Curies and Henri Becquerel share Nobel prize in physics for the discovery of radioactivity. Marie also gets her Ph.D. in science. The Curies are not impressed with the fancy dinners and are even less impressed with the snoopiness of reporters. They become public figures overnight with publicity such as a cartoon character called "Professor Radium," a racehorse named "Marie Curie," and reporters spying on their cat, Didi.

1914 Opens Institute of Radium in Paris. In 1932 opens one in Poland too.

1906 Pierre gets run over by a horse-drawn cart, killing him instantly. Although he is already dying due to the damaging effects of radiation, the cart speeds things up. His death becomes a turning point in Curie's career. She is the first woman offered a professorship at the Sorbonne. She accepts, taking Pierre's place.

1921 Visits United States and receives a chunk of radium from President Harding. She likes the U.S. so much she visits again 5 years later.

1914–18 Organizes X-ray service for French army during World War I. Since you can see through skin with x-rays, they are useful in finding metal shrapnel and broken bones. Curie has several big cars rigged up with X-ray machines and taken to the front lines so the wounded can receive quick attention.

1934 Curie is overexposed. She may be dead, but she may glow forever.

HOW AN X-RAY MACHINE WORKS

Basically, an X-ray is a beam of energy powerful enough to go through light material—such as your flesh—but not go through heavier material such as bones and metal. The beams that make it through get recorded on photographic film, leaving a shadow of your bones or whatever else blocks those beams. Let's see how an X-ray machine works.

Tungsten Target

High voltage Power supply

Window

X-ray beam

Electrons shoot off from a heated filament. When these electrons crash into the surface of tungsten and excite the tungsten atoms, the atoms give off X-rays. The tungsten target is angled so that the X-rays come out of a window in the lead box, through your hand, and onto the film.

X-ray image of bone

Film

BEAM YOUR HAND

Shine a flashlight through your hand in a dark room. Visible, safe photons of light penetrate your thinner skin and soft tissue allowing you to see a dark area where your bones are.

Like light, **X-rays** are made up of packets of energy. The difference is that **X-rays** have more energy than light packets and have a wavelength our eyes can't see. Still, they can be recorded on photographic paper.

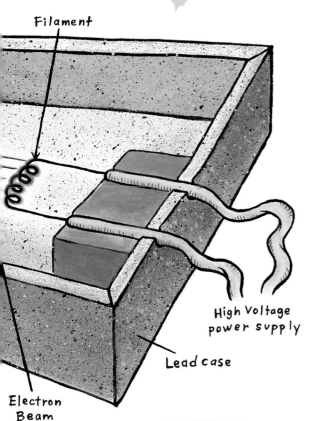

Limited exposure to radiation is OK, but too much can make you sick. Because of this, people who work with radiation (X-ray technicians, for example) keep a piece of X-ray film on their name tag. The film is developed periodically to see how much radiation the person has been exposed to. If it turns black, indicating a lot of exposure, he or she does a different job for a while and may need to see a doctor.

To block X-rays, workers wear lead aprons. You probably wear one when your dentist takes X-rays of your teeth, keeping you from unnecessary exposure to radiation. With todays technology, X-rays emit far lower doses of radiation than in the past.

Filament

High Voltage power supply

Lead case

Electron Beam

⚡ USES FOR REAL AND ⚡ ARTIFICIAL RADIOACTIVITY

- Airport security uses X-rays to scan suitcases at the airport

- Determining the ages of rocks and fossils

- Making glow-in-the-dark watches and paint

- Finding cracks in heavy machinery and airplanes

- Sterilizing medical tools and devices

- The process of preserving certain foods by destroying food-spoiling bacteria has been approved, but is not yet a common practice

RADIATION IN MEDICINE:
The Good News and the Bad News

Bad news first:

Radiation attacks growth centers, such as where bones or red blood cells are growing. Leukemia, the destruction of bone marrow, can be caused by overexposure to radiation. Both Curie and her daughter Irene were exposed to large amounts of radiation and eventually died of leukemia.

Good news:

Cancer is the rapid growth of abnormal cells. If the same radiation that attacks growth cells is pointed at the uncontrolled growing cancer cells, it can kill those cells and stop their growth.

Albert Einstein
Born: March 14, 1879; Ulm, Germany
DEAD: April 18, 1955
Famous because: He developed theories of relativity and the photoelectric effect—among others—which greatly influenced many areas of science.

BORN
1879

1890

1900

1895 Fails entrance exam to Institute of Technology in Zurich, Switzerland.

1891 At 12 years old, Einstein studies differential and integral calculus.

1901 Becomes Swiss citizen. Is declared unfit for the Swiss army because of flat feet and varicose veins. (He may be smart, but he's not perfect.)

1903 Marries Mileva Maric, his physics-loving sweetheart.

48

Einstein didn't start out as the brightest pebble on the beach. However, in his lifetime he was recognized as one of the most creative intellects in human history. His theories—including the famous E=mc² equation—changed the way we look at space, time, movement, gravity, and matter. In college he was said to be clever, but stubborn. He was a loner, yet developed deep, lifelong friendships with some heavy-duty thinkers. He was also considered somewhat of an eccentric. It is rumored that he stopped wearing socks once he calculated how much time it took to put on and remove them.

In later life, he got into working for peace and social justice in addition to physics. His energy-mass equation (E=mc²) states that a small amount of matter can be changed into enormous amounts of energy. It was very disturbing to him that this theory was applied to the creation of the atomic and hydrogen bombs, the most destructive weapons ever known.

1905 A big year for Einstein. He gets his doctorate degree and publishes three articles in a German physics magazine. These articles—on heat, the photoelectric effect, and the theory of special relativity (nothing too heavy)—change our view of the universe forever.
One is on Brownian motion, which is the mechanics of heat. The second, the photoelectric effect, concerns the interaction of light and matter. This theory is based on the idea that light energy travels in packets called photons, instead of in a continual flow or stream.
The third predicts that when traveling close to the speed of light relative to an observer, objects gain mass, age slower, and shrink in the direction of travel. This theory introduces the famous E= mc² equation.

1939 Einstein signs a letter encouraging President Roosevelt to build the atomic bomb. He has gotten word that the uranium atom has been split and that the Germans are building an atomic bomb. He knows that the United States has to do it first because Hitler, a very dangerous leader, is in power. Building the atomic bomb becomes known as the Manhattan Project, but Einstein never works on it himself.

1955 Einstein runs out of energy—or did he run out of matter? Oh, what does it matter? He's dead.

DEAD

1910   **1920**   **1930**   **1940**

1909 Hypothesizes that light can behave as both waves and particles. Einstein gets his first honorary doctorate degree from the University of Zurich. Over his lifetime he receives over fifteen such degrees from universities including London, Cambridge, Glasgow, Harvard, and Princeton without ever having to go to classes.

1919 Marries his cousin Elsa Lowenthal, who is more into the niceties of life than he is. She sees that he is not interrupted while he works. Einstein never really finds the love of his life.

1933 The Nazis have taken up the practice of oppressing Jews by throwing them in jail or concentration camps and killing them. On a hunch, the Einsteins, who were Jews, leave Germany for the United States, never to return again. The Nazis, angry with Einstein for denouncing his German citizenship, ransack his summer home and take his sailboat.

1907 Einstein is refused a job as lecturer at University of Berne with the excuse that his paper on relativity was not understandable.

1918 After a forced separation due to WWI, Einstein and Mileva get divorced.

1921 Wins Nobel Prize in physics. Many physics professionals feel he deserves one for his work in relativity, but Einstein still has work to do on that theory. Since they don't want to wait any longer, he wins the prize for his work on the photoelectric effect.

1945 "The war is won, but peace is not," says Einstein. Very upset about the atomic bomb dropped on Hiroshima, Einstein pushes for a world government.

E=mc²: WHAT DOES IT MEAN?

Let's start with the letters:

E stands for *energy*—the capacity to do work or to move stuff.

M stands for *mass*—stuff that weighs something.

C stands for the *speed of light*. Light always travels at about 186,000 miles per second. C actually stands for *constant*, because the speed of light doesn't change when traveling in a vacuum, like space.

2 stands for *squared*. To square a number you multiply that number by itself.
For example: $3^2 = 3 \times 3$, which equals 9.

C² or (c x c) is the speed of light multiplied by itself. That's a big number. Before Einstein came along, people used to think that energy was energy and that matter was matter. But, with a lot of deep thought, Einstein figured out that energy and matter are interchangeable. So if you could change matter, or stuff, into energy, you'd get a whole lot of energy. For example, let's plug a pastrami sandwich into our equation $E = mc^2$.

LOTS of Energy

E (energy) = Mass (pastrami sandwich) x C^2 (186,000 x 186,000) = a BIG number.
If you could actually change a pastrami sandwich into energy you'd probably get enough energy to power every city in America for at least 5 days.
You could drive a car around the world about 180,000 times.
You could run a room air conditioner for at least 500,000 years.

So $E = mc^2$ tells us how much energy you can get from stuff if you could convert that stuff into energy.

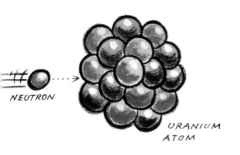

NEUTRON

URANIUM
ATOM

Einstein's theory about energy coming from matter happens in a process called *fission*. Fission occurs when a tiny atom of uranium or plutonium is split in two by a particle—a neutron—which comes screaming at it, traveling up to 12,000 miles a second, releasing enormous amounts of energy.

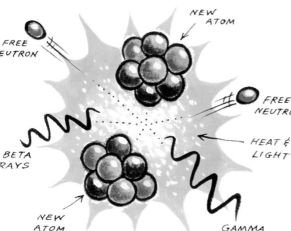

NEW
ATOM

FREE
NEUTRON

FREE
NEUTRON

BETA
RAYS

NEW
ATOM

HEAT &
LIGHT

GAMMA
RAYS

KA-BOOM!

When uranium splits, we get two smaller atoms and two free neutrons, which zoom off to split more uranium atoms.

All these pieces weigh less than what we started with. The missing mass was changed into heat energy, also releasing dangerous radiation waves. This can happen slowly in a nuclear reactor (making electricity), or quickly in an atomic bomb.

QUOTES FROM AL

"Great spirits have always found violent opposition from mediocre minds."

"The important thing is not to stop questioning."

"The process of scientific discovery is, in effect, a continual flight of wonder."

E = MC²

Name: Robert Hutchings Goddard
Born: October 5, 1882; Worcester, Massachusetts
DEAD: August 10, 1945
Famous because: He invented the rocket.

BORN
1882

1890

1900

1910

1899 While avoiding his farm work by hanging out in the branches of a cherry tree, Goddard gazes into the sky and is struck with a vision of traveling into outer space. "I was a different boy when I decended that ladder," he says later. This dream becomes his life's work and obsession.

1908 Goddard begins his career in physics at Clark University in Worcester, Massachusetts. He eventually earns his Ph.D. and teaches physics.

1898 H. G. Wells's space-fiction novel *War of the Worlds* sparks young Goddard's imagination about constructing a workable space-flight machine.

1904 At age 22, Goddard graduates from high school. (So, he's a late bloomer.)

1912 Wonders if it is possible to use rocket power to get to and travel in space. He figures that conventional solid fuels, such as compressed gun powder, aren't powerful enough and they require oxygen to burn, which is unavailable in the vacuum of space. He therefore experiments with fuels made from hydrogen and oxygen.

52

Goddard is considered the father of modern rocketry when, in fact, he didn't get near the recognition he deserved while he was alive. How much can you enjoy your fame when you're dead?

Goddard received 83 patents on rocket- and space-related devices during his lifetime, and his estate patented over 131 ideas from his journals after his death. (At least *someone* got rich off his ideas.) In 1960 the United States government made a million-dollar settlement with Goddard's 43-year-old wife Ester and the Guggenheim Foundation for the use of his patents after he died. Part of the settlement went to starting the Goddard Memorial Library at Clark University in Worcester, Massachusetts.

Goddard was ridiculed and teased for his rocket ideas. He did most of his research alone or with a small group of trusted followers, but he was so convinced that space travel was possible that he kept trying in spite of the obstacles. Among his successes were pumps for rocket fuel, self-cooling rocket motors, variable-thrust rocket engines (which allow the pilot to control the rocket's speed), and practical rocket-landing devices. He also designed rocket engines for the Intermediate Range Ballistic Missile (IRBM) in 1940, many years before they were used. The Atlas, Thor, Jupiter, and Redstone missiles used similar rocket engines. Today, virtually every facet of rocketry uses at least one of Goddard's patents.

1932 Goddard develops *gyroscopic stabilization* for rocket flight. A gyro is a small top that keeps pointing in the same direction no matter how its support is tilted. It is the heart of all rocket guidance systems keeping a rocket on course without outside help. This steering system will be used well into the 21st century.

1917 The United States enters World War I. Goddard makes war rockets that work like high-explosive machine guns.

1920–1925 In the secrecy of his lab, Goddard develops a rocket motor using liquid fuels (liquid oxygen and gasoline).

1935 Goddard launches the first liquid-fuel rocket that travels faster than Mach 1, the speed of sound.

1918 Develops and demonstrates the bazooka, a handheld rocket launcher later used in World War II.

1929 Goes up like a rocket, comes down with a big fiery crash. Fire marshall bans tests on Aunt Effie's farm.

DEAD

1920

1930

1940

1915 Demonstrates that a rocket can travel more efficiently in a vacuum than in the air. This is because there is no air resistance in a vacuum to slow it down.

1919–1920 The Smithsonian Institution publishes his book, *A Method of Reaching Extreme Altitudes,* which describes the theory of rocket propulsion. The newspapers hang Goddard out to dry. He receives public ridicule, is called an impractical dreamer and "Moon Man." Goddard goes into hiding.

1926 The Big Day. The first liquid-fuel rocket is launched from Aunt Effie's farm in Auburn, Massachusetts. It rises 41 feet in 2 1/2 seconds and travels 184 feet. It only gets a little bit of liftoff, but, hey, it's good enough for Aunt Effie.

1930 Charles Lindbergh, the first pilot to fly solo across the Atlantic, hears that Goddard got kicked off Aunt Effie's farm. He gets $100,000 from the Guggenheim Foundation for Goddard to set up a rocket research lab in Roswell, New Mexico.

1945 Goddard is propelled out of this world. 5,4,3,2,1 Blast off! Bye-bye!

BLAST OFF!

HOW A ROCKET ENGINE WORKS

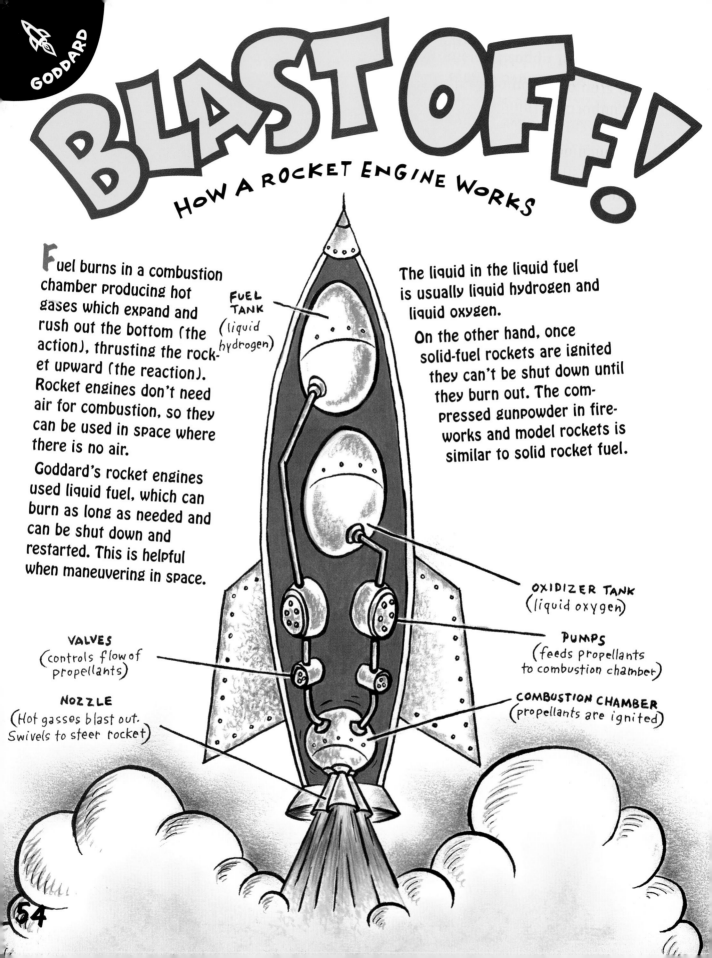

Fuel burns in a combustion chamber producing hot gases which expand and rush out the bottom (the action), thrusting the rocket upward (the reaction). Rocket engines don't need air for combustion, so they can be used in space where there is no air.

Goddard's rocket engines used liquid fuel, which can burn as long as needed and can be shut down and restarted. This is helpful when maneuvering in space.

The liquid in the liquid fuel is usually liquid hydrogen and liquid oxygen.

On the other hand, once solid-fuel rockets are ignited they can't be shut down until they burn out. The compressed gunpowder in fireworks and model rockets is similar to solid rocket fuel.

FUEL TANK
(liquid hydrogen)

OXIDIZER TANK
(liquid oxygen)

VALVES
(controls flow of propellants)

PUMPS
(feeds propellants to combustion chamber)

NOZZLE
(Hot gasses blast out. Swivels to steer rocket)

COMBUSTION CHAMBER
(propellants are ignited)

A rocket engine is a basic demonstration of Newton's third law of motion, which states that for every action there is an equal and opposite reaction. In a rocket, fuel is burned and forced out the bottom—that's the action. The rocket being propelled through the sky or space by the force of the fuel is the reaction.

Blow up an ordinary balloon. When you let go, what happens? The balloon puts pressure on the air inside it. The *action* is that the air rushes out. The *reaction* is that the balloon is propelled forward and flies all over the place.

SPACE TRAVEL TODAY

The space shuttle uses five rocket engines to get it into space. It has two solid-fuel boosters and three large liquid-fuel engines, both of which boost the rocket out of the earth's atmosphere. Once it's in space, smaller liquid-fuel engines are used to fly and maneuver the shuttle.

I send them to the moon and they never ever thank me.

Name: Louis Semour Bazett Leakey
Born: August 7, 1903; Kabete, Kenya
DEAD: October 1, 1972; London, England
Famous because: Discovered oldest human fossils so far

1933–35 Leaves his first wife Frida, who is not into this fossil stuff. Meets Mary Douglas Nicol, a geology student studying prehistory. Her mom thinks Leakey's flaky, but Mary marries him anyway.

1922 Studies anthropology at Cambridge University.

BORN
1903

1910   1920   1930

1903 Louis Leakey—the first white baby to become a member of the Kikuyu people. All came to stare at him and spit on him. This tribal ritual is "the saliva of peace," but his mom is right there with a sponge. He is the spitting image of his dad.

1916 In Leakey's library: Charles Darwin's *Origin of a Species* (1860), which explains how humans evolved from ape-like ancestors, and his *The Descent of Man* (1871) in which he writes that the missing link to human ancestry existed in Africa. At age 13, Leakey decides to find out if Darwin was right. Finds tools made of obsidian—shiny glass-like rock.

1919–1921 Leakey is sent to an English prep school. His proper British schoolmates laugh at the uncouth white African, knock him down to size, and lock him in a coal hole.

LEAKEY: The Dead Guys' Dead Guy

Leakey thought Africa might be the cradle of humanity and set out to test his theory. He made many significant discoveries of fossils and artifacts in East Africa that date humankind back more than a million years. As paleoanthropologists, scientists who study fossils of people, Leakey and his wife Mary have greatly changed the way we humans look at our own origin.

Leakey's parents went to Kenya, Africa with the Church Missionary Society to teach the natives about Christianity. The Leakeys respected African culture and made sure their children learned the native way of life. Louis grew up among the African children, teaching them barefoot football and wearing very few clothes. At age 13 he was formally initiated as a member of the Kikuyu people.

Being an paleoanthropologist is like being a detective. You have to always keep an open mind and be prepared for the unexpected. Popular thought held that humans inhabited North America as far back as about 1,000 B.C. Leakey, however, believed that "Man must have been in the Americas at least as long ago as 15,000 B.C." And Leakey didn't stop there. In 1963 Leakey started digging in California, looking for evidence that humans existed more than 50,000 years ago! He died before he could find conclusive evidence, so if you are inclined to be a paleoanthropologist, start digging—you could help piece the puzzle of human origin together.

1959: Nutcracker Man Found in Olduvai Gorge

Olduvai (ALL-du-vye) Gorge is a rocky valley in Tanzania (tan-zan-EE-ah), Africa, where the who's who of skeletons lay to rest. Leakey's first trip in 1931 unearthed stone tools that gave evidence of the existence of humans 1.6 million years ago. In 1959, he made his most famous find, zinjanthropus (or Nutcracker Man) and claimed the gorilla-looking skull with viselike jaws (hence, his nickname) was a distant cousin to humans. (Mary actually found the skull, but her husband got the credit.) Nutcracker Man, a hominid (man-ape) fossil, is believed to be 1,750,000 years old. Leakey richly earned a reputation for being wild and going against convention. His unorthodox methods of archaeology often had the scientific community up in arms. Many scientists were even more steamed because he was so successful.

"This fish has been dead way longer than I have."

DEAD 1972

Timeline

1940

1945 World War II. To help out, Leakey puts his research on hold and works for the Criminal Investigation Department in Nairobi to help solve murders. He's into both freshly dead and *way* dead!

1947–1959 Second wife Mary Douglas Nicol discovers the most complete skull of *Proconsul africanus*, a primate with enough hominid traits to suggest that humans started at least 25 million years ago. A major breakthrough!

1950

1950 Son Richard, 6 years old, is sent off to play and digs up the bone of an extinct pig twice the size of both a warthog and an African forest pig.

1957 Beginning of lifelong friendship and sponsorship of Jane Goodall's research on chimpanzees.

1960

1961 Leakey unearths the fossil of *Homo habilis*, which he believes to be a nearly 2-million-year-old direct ancestor of the *Homo sapiens*—or human. That's us!

1970

1972 Leakey's a future fossil— he's stone cold.

1972 Richard Leakey discovers another hominid skull near Lake Rudolf, Kenya. It is estimated at 2.6 million years old and appears to be an even more direct ancestor of man.

What's a Fossil?

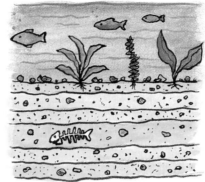

Fossils are clues to the mysteries of our planet's past. They make up the unwritten history of life on earth by telling us about the plants and animals that existed long before we got here. Fossils can be bones or teeth—in which the original material has been replaced by minerals and stone—or they can be footprints or impressions of animals or plants that were left in soft mud or sand and later changed into stone.

Fossils are made when plants or animals are buried quickly in sediment— such as the mud and sand that collects at the bottom of lakes, rivers, oceans, and swamps. After millions of years, more sediment collects on top of the buried plant or animal and presses down so hard that the sediments at the bottom are turned to rock (that's why this kind of rock is called sedimentary rock). Minerals help cement the sediment together.

RAMAPITHECUS

AUSTRALOPITHECUS

HOMO HABILIS

HOMO ERECTUS

AFRICA

This is the area in which the Leakeys did most of their research and found the oldest human bones so far.

GEOLOGICAL TIMELINE

	PRE-CAMBRIAN	PALEOZOIC						MESOZOIC			CENOZOIC		ERA
		Cambrian	Ordovician	Silurian	Devonian	Carboniferous	Permian	Triassic	Jurassic	Cretaceous	Tertiary	Quaternary	PERIOD
	One Cell Life	Amphibians Invertebrates		Fish				Reptiles Dinosaurs			Mammals Birds	Humans	WHO'S ALIVE
	600			230						65	3	0	MILLIONS OF YEARS AGO

↑ EXTINCTION OF DINOSAURS

Is it HUMAN or NOT?

THREE WAYS TO KNOW YOU'RE NOT AN APE

1. Humans walk upright. Apes, related to humans, lean over and have very long arms.

2. Humans use tools. Refined stone tools indicate that the creature used his or her mind and hands to create and use tools.

3. Humans can create art. Mary Leakey found 1,500-year-old rock paintings in Tanzania depicting the lives of the late stone age people.

NEANDERTHAL MAN

CRO-MAGNON MAN

BEAKMAN

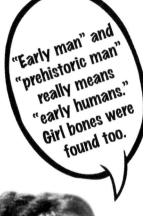

"Early man" and "prehistoric man" really means "early humans." Girl bones were found too.

Tools for Fossilhounds:

dentist pick
hammer   hand lens
knapsack   brush
notebook and pencil
goggles   speciman bag
newspaper
magnifying glass

Stone age cave art

59

Name: Philo Taylor Farnsworth
Born: August 19, 1906; Beaver, Utah
DEAD: March 11, 1971
Famous because: He invented important parts of the electronic television.

1920 Comes up with the idea for the television. While plowing some Idaho fields into nice straight rows, he is struck with an inspiration. "I can scan a picture that way, by taking the dots, the electrons, back and forth as you would read a page." He's 14 years old.

1925 Graduates from Brigham Young University in Salt Lake City, Utah. Investors give Farnsworth $25,000 in research money. By the time a quality picture is achieved, several years later, investors will have ponied up over one million dollars for Farnsworth's research. Also in 1925 the first mechanical televisions are demonstrated in the United States (by Charles Francis Jenkins) and in England (by John Logie Baird).

BORN 1906

1910

1920

1930

1912 Philo, at 6 years old, declares that he will become an inventor.

1921 With no formal training in electronics or radio broadcasting, college freshman Farnsworth logically diagrams how he plans to transmit and receive images over distances of many miles. His teachers are blown away. This also is the same year that the National Broadcasting Company (NBC) comes into existence.

1918 Wins $25 in a building contest from a magazine. Buys his first long pants.

1930 First movies on TV. Farnsworth experiments with some bootleg movie clips of a hockey game, the Dempsey-Tunney fight at Philadelphia, and Mary Pickford brushing her hair in *The Taming of the Shrew*.

ow who, you may ask, is Philo T. Farnsworth and what is he doing in this book of famous dead guys and gals? That, being of the scientific mind that you have (or you wouldn't be reading this book in the first place), is a very legitimate question. Not every scientist was as profound as Einstein, and not every inventor was as prolific as Edison. Some people made significant scientific contributions and received little or no recognition for their efforts. One such individual is Philo T. Farnsworth, inventor of the electronic television.

Electronic Television Comes of Age

By 1927, many people had experimented with the television. At age 21, Farnsworth demonstrated a working model of a television system. His image dissector transmitted an image by dividing it into dots and then restoring it to form a copy of the original image. Farnsworth's image dissector, his major claim to fame, worked far better than Zworykin's system for picture quality. This brought TV out of the lab and into people's homes.

ELECTRONIC TV BEATS OUT MECHANICAL TV

The mechanical television was demonstrated in England and the United States in 1925. It worked like a cartoon in which whole pictures were shown quickly in succession, creating an illusion of movement. The process is slow, requires big, clunky equipment, and at its best, the image is blurry and lacks detail.

Electronic television is made possible by the way electrons (tiny charged particles) behave in a vacuum. In an airtight tube, the flow of electrons creates an electron beam, which is the critical part of electronic television.

DEAD 1971

1940

1950

1960

1937 Agreement is signed by the Farnsworth Television and Radio Corporation and AT&T (American Telephone & Telegraph) allowing each to use the other's patents.

1939 Electronic television sets for home use go on sale at the World's Fair in New York City, but nobody buys them. There are only a few broadcasting companies, so not all homes could receive TV signals. A television set costs from $200 to $1,000—a lot of money in 1939. It costs a nickel to see a movie at the theater.

1945 Vladimir Zworykin (Philo's closest competitor in the race for the perfect TV picture) invents the *image orthicon camera* which is 100 times more sensitive to light than the old TV cameras. This gives a much clearer picture without the need for hot lights during production.

1947 The first televised World Series baseball games. Without TVs in their own homes, people go to their local watering hole to see the games. The TV epidemic spreads quickly after the World Series and TV sales skyrocket.

1951 The first recorded situation comedy (that is, not broadcast live), "I Love Lucy," becomes an overnight sensation.

1956 Farnsworth is granted a patent for a storage-type cathode-ray tube. A cathode-ray tube is a glass tube in which electric current, passing through the tube, makes the tube glow. It is the most important part of the TV receiver.

1962 The first privately built and owned satellite, Telstar, transmits TV pictures from Europe. This is such a big deal that a rock and roll group called the Tornadoes names a song after the satellite.

1971 Farnsworth blows his picture tube.

Beam Me Up, Philo!

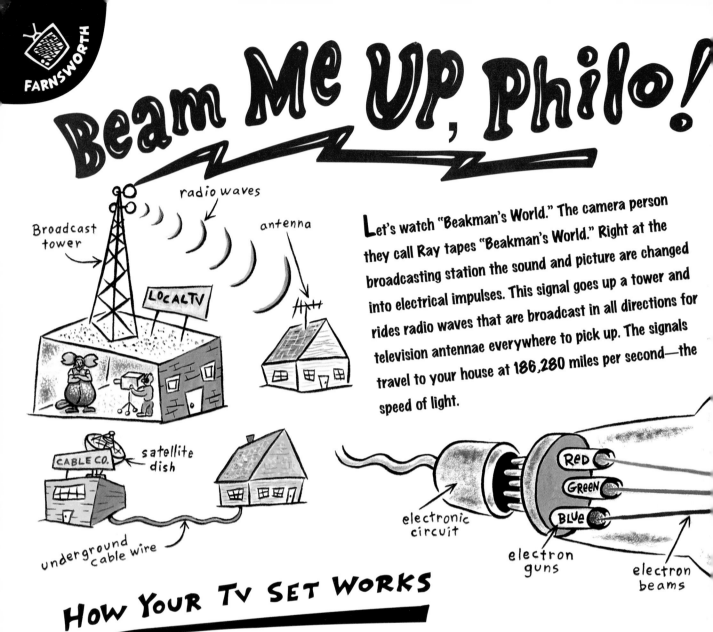

FARNSWORTH

radio waves

Broadcast tower

LOCAL TV

antenna

CABLE CO.

satellite dish

underground cable wire

electronic circuit

RED
GREEN
BLUE

electron guns

electron beams

Let's watch "Beakman's World." The camera person they call Ray tapes "Beakman's World." Right at the broadcasting station the sound and picture are changed into electrical impulses. This signal goes up a tower and rides radio waves that are broadcast in all directions for television antennae everywhere to pick up. The signals travel to your house at 186,280 miles per second—the speed of light.

How Your TV Set Works

If you have cable TV, the signal is sent by wire to a cable company where it travels to your house by an underground wire. Once at your house, the signals from the radio waves or cable are turned back into electricity and finally into a picture on your TV set.

Your television is the receiver that picks up the channel of your choice. The cathode-ray tube, or picture tube, is where all the action happens, and is the part of the black-and-white TV picture that Farnsworth perfected.

In a color TV, there are three electron guns—one for red, one for green, and one for blue—at one end of the tube. Electron beams are shot to the other end of the tube, and pass through a metal plate with lots of holes in it. The three color beams go through each hole onto a screen that contains many *phosphors*—dots that light up either red, blue, or green. The combination of the different colored phosphors makes a sharp color image.

PERSISTENCE OF VISION

Quickly wiggle your index finger back and forth. What you are seeing is *persistence of vision*, which happens when an image stays in your eye for longer than you are seeing it. **TV** is made up of lots of still pictures that, when flashed quickly in front of you, look like a moving image.

FARNSWORTH

picture tube

mask

phosphor dot screen

This TV image was created one dot at a time. A TV will fill up, or scan, the whole screen with dots in 1/30 of a second. So every second you are seeing thirty different images.